England and Spain in action in the final of Euro 2024!

WELCOME!

WHAT AN AMAZING YEAR of football it's been! Full of drama, excitement and incredible achievements. Join us as we take a look back at the biggest moments and celebrate the heroes of the game. Enjoy the book!

GARY

WHAT'S IN YOUR 2025 ANNUAL?

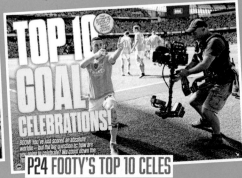

THE BIG WINNERS OF 2024!

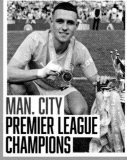

MAN. CITY PREMIER LEAGUE CHAMPIONS

CITY CLAIMED a record-breaking fourth title in a row, and a sixth in seven years — pipping Arsenal on the final day!

MAN. UNITED FA CUP WINNERS

CITY'S DOUBLE hopes were shattered by Manchester rivals United, who ran out shock 2-1 winners at Wembley!

REAL MADRID CHAMPIONS LEAGUE WINNERS

JUDE BELLINGHAM helped Real win their 15th Champions League title — beating Borussia Dortmund 2-0 in the final!

ERLING HAALAND PREMIER LEAGUE GOLDEN BOOT

HAALAND'S 27 goals in 31 games saw him finish as top scorer for the second year in a row!

LIVERPOOL EFL CUP WINNERS

JURGEN KLOPP'S final trophy as Liverpool manager, thanks to Virgil van Dijk's extra-time winner over Chelsea!

96 PAGES *OF FOOTY FUN!*

P62 25 FOOTY THINGS TO DO IN 2025

P84 MBAPPE MANIA

LEGENDARY NO.10 POSTERS!

We celebrate the most iconic shirt number with 13 legends who famously wore it!

THE LOL! ZONE!

IF BALLERS WERE DOGGIES!

MOHAMED SALAH IS A... POODLE

ANTOINE GRIEZMANN IS A... CHINESE CRESTED DOG

ILKAY GUNDOGAN IS A... PUG

MARC CUCURELLA IS A... POODLE

LUKA MODRIC IS A... CHINESE CRESTED DOG

PEPE IS A... BOXER

MARTIN ODEGAARD IS A... LHASA APSO

JACK GREALISH IS A... YORKSHIRE TERRIER

DESIGN A BADGE FOR...

DOGGY FC!

IMAGINE THESE guys all play for Doggy FC — what would their badge look like?

Diego
MARADONA
ARGENTINA

No.
10
Icon

BADGES & ANIMALS!

On which club's badge would you find these *LITTLE CRITTERS*? Good luck!

1
A Ipswich
B West Brom
C Birmingham

2
A Derby
B Portsmouth
C Oxford

3
A Leicester
B Hull
C Wolves

4
A Newcastle
B Middlesbrough
C Gillingham

5
A Cardiff
B Brighton
C Swansea

6
A Aston Villa
B Millwall
C Doncaster

7
A Bristol City
B Wigan
C Norwich

8
A Leeds
B Sunderland
C Aston Villa

9
A Watford
B Mansfield
C QPR

YOUR FOOTY BRAIN POWER

YOUR SCORE ☐ /9

9 GENIUS
7 PROFESSIONAL
5 SEMI-PRO
3 AMATEUR
1 SUNDAY LEAGUE
0 OH NO, DISASTER

ANSWERS ON PAGE 92!

9

20 YEARS OF LIONEL

1,069 games 838 goals

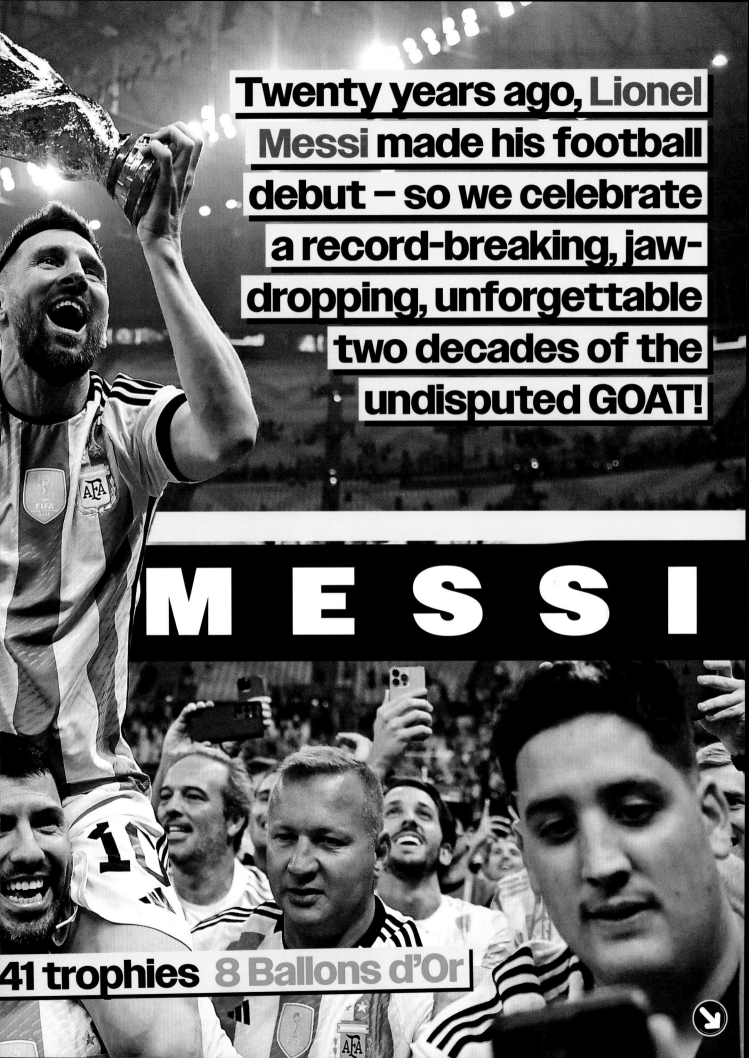

Twenty years ago, Lionel Messi made his football debut – so we celebrate a record-breaking, jaw-dropping, unforgettable two decades of the undisputed GOAT!

MESSI

41 trophies **8 Ballons d'Or**

■ Three years after moving to Spain, Leo makes his debut for Barcelona, aged 17, in a La Liga match against city rivals Espanyol...

2004

200

2005

■ Becomes Argentina's youngest-ever player at a World Cup when he comes on as sub — and scores — against Serbia and Montenegro in a 6-0 win...

■ Messi scores his first-ever goal for Barcelona — a cheeky lob against Albacete...

6

Helps Argentina to footballing gold at the Beijing Olympics — pictured here with ex-Man. City star Sergio Aguero...

2008

2007

Scores a sensational solo goal against Getafe — dribbling from his own half, beating four defenders and rounding the keeper, before rolling the ball into the empty net...

■ Leads Barcelona to another league title, scores FOUR in one game against Arsenal and wins the European Golden Shoe for the first time...

2010

2009

■ Wins his first Ballon d'Or after a remarkable year – which included a La Liga, Copa del Rey and Champions League treble...

NEL MESSI

Sets a staggering world record by scoring 91 (yes, NINETY-ONE!) goals in a calendar year, confirming his status as the greatest ever...

2012

2011

Scores a 20-yard banger against Man. United in the Champions League Final at Wembley as Barcelona win 3-1 — his third UCL medal...

2013

Claims another La Liga title with Barcelona, wins another Golden Boot — and gets Ballon d'Or number four...

2014

Smashes the all-time La Liga scoring record of 251 goals when he nets a hat-trick against Sevilla...

2015

Leads Barcelona to another treble of La Liga, Copa del Rey and the Champions League — his fourth UCL winner's medal...

■ Becomes the first player to score 300 La Liga goals — and picks up a record fifth Ballon d'Or...

016

■ Breaks Gerd Muller's long-standing record for most goals (366) in a single top European league — and wins a record fifth European Golden Shoe...

2018

© FC Barcelona Autor Santi Garcés

2017

■ Scores his 500th career goal for Barcelona and claims a record-equalling fourth European Golden Shoe...

■ Secures a record sixth Ballon d'Or after yet another La Liga and Golden Shoe-winning season...

2019

2021

2020

■ Scores his 644th goal for Barcelona, overtaking Pele as the player with the most goals scored for a single club...

■ A huge year for Leo — he sensationally quits Barcelona to join PSG; he wins the Copa America with Argentina, his first major international trophy; and he claims a record seventh Ballon d'Or...

■ After winning his second Ligue I title with PSG, he moves to Inter Miami in the USA, where he wins the Leagues Cup — oh, and he wins Ballon d'Or number eight...

2023

2022

2024

■ Captains Argentina to another Copa America victory — their second in a row. It's trophy number 4l for the greatest footballer of all time! What will 2025 have in store for Leo?

■ Leads Argentina to World Cup victory in Qatar — and is named player of the tournament...

A YEAR IN FOOTBALL!

How much can you remember about FOOTY IN 2024? Let's find out!

1 Who did Real Madrid beat in the Champions League final in June?
- A Bayern Munich
- B Borussia Dortmund
- C PSG

2 Who won last season's EFL Cup back in February?
- A Liverpool
- B Chelsea
- C Newcastle

3 Who was the top scorer in the WSL last season?
- A Alessia Russo
- B Khadija Shaw
- C Ella Toone

4 Who won the European Golden Shoe last season?
- A Kylian Mbappe
- B Harry Kane
- C Erling Haaland

5 Which Championship club made the 2023-24 FA Cup semi-final?
- A Blackburn
- B Preston
- C Coventry

6 Which club won the Bundesliga last season?
- A Bayern Munich
- B Borussia Dortmund
- C Bayer Leverkusen

7 Who was the 2023-24 Premier League Player of the Season?
- A Ollie Watkins
- B Phil Foden
- C Declan Rice

8 Who did England beat in the semi-final of Euro 2024?
- A Netherlands
- B France
- C Switzerland

9 Oliver Glasner became manager of which club in February?
- A Brighton
- B Bournemouth
- C Crystal Palace

YOUR FOOTY BRAIN POWER

YOUR SCORE ☐/9

- 9 GENIUS
- 7 PROFESSIONAL
- 5 SEMI-PRO
- 3 AMATEUR
- 1 SUNDAY LEAGUE
- 0 OH NO, DISASTER

ANSWERS ON PAGE 92!

WAYNE
ROO
NEY

2003-18
120 caps /
53 goals

ENGLAND

No.
10
Icon

BBC

MATCH
OF THE
DAY
MAGAZINE

If you love footy, then you'll love Match of the Day magazine!

ON SALE EVERY FORTNIGHT!

BBC

MATCH OF THE DAY

THE PREMIER LEAGUE IS BACK!

THE **BIG** 2024-25 **KICK-OFF!**

EVERY CLUB RATED ★ STAR MEN ★ TACTICS ★ SIGNINGS ★ PREDICTIONS

Who wants this, then?

PLUS! EFL CHAMPIONSHIP ● LEAGUE ONE ● LEAGUE TWO ● SPFL

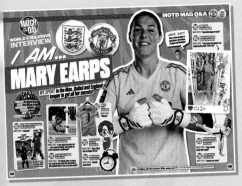

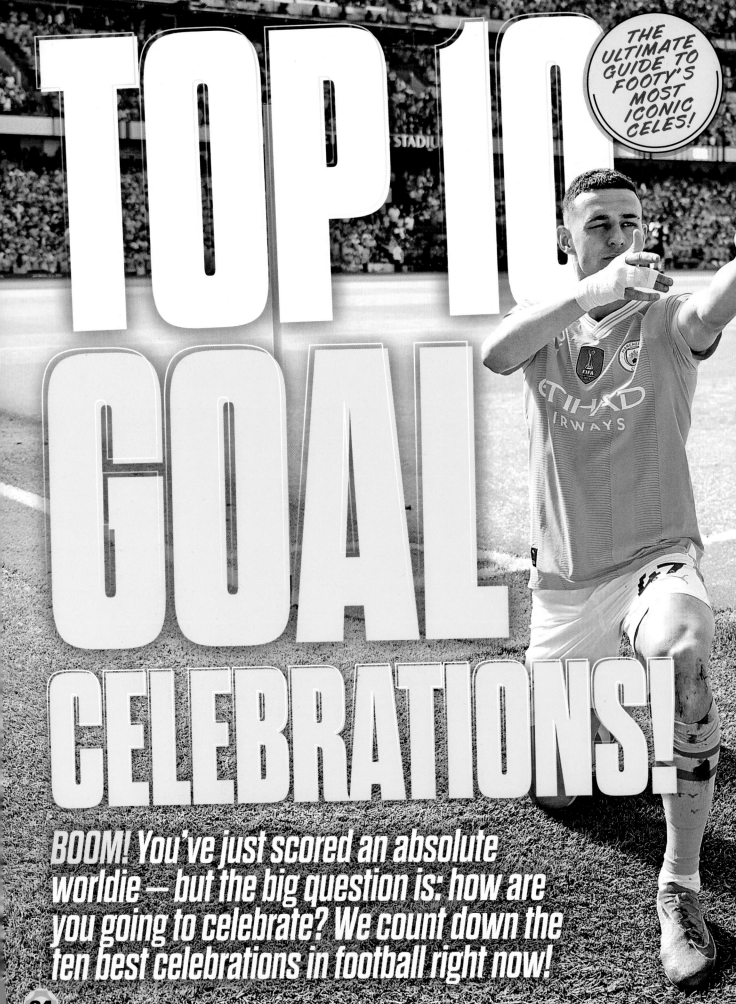

TOP 10 GOAL CELEBRATIONS!

BOOM! You've just scored an absolute worldie — but the big question is: how are you going to celebrate? We count down the ten best celebrations in football right now!

THE GOGGLES
10 JOHN MCGINN

ICONIC RATING	★☆☆☆☆	MY RATING
DIFFICULTY RATING	★★★★☆	
STYLE RATING	★☆☆☆☆	/10
FUN RATING	★★★★☆	

THE FIST BUMP
ROBERT LEWANDOWSKI

9

ICONIC RATING	★★☆☆☆	MY RATING
DIFFICULTY RATING	★★☆☆☆	
STYLE RATING	★★☆☆☆	/10
FUN RATING	★★★☆☆	

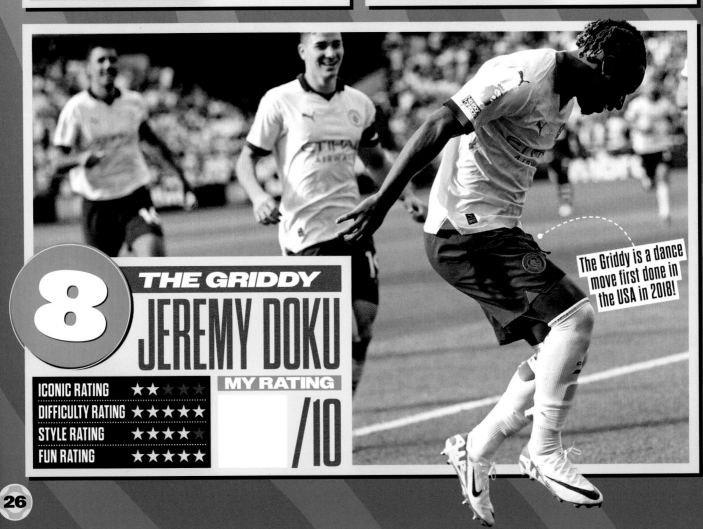

8 THE GRIDDY
JEREMY DOKU

ICONIC RATING	★★☆☆☆	MY RATING
DIFFICULTY RATING	★★★★★	
STYLE RATING	★★★★☆	/10
FUN RATING	★★★★★	

The Griddy is a dance move first done in the USA in 2018!

Bukayo Saka has also done this celebration!

THE TEMPLE POINT

MARCUS RASHFORD

		MY RATING
ICONIC RATING	★★★☆☆	
DIFFICULTY RATING	★★☆☆☆	/10
STYLE RATING	★★★★☆	
FUN RATING	★★☆☆☆	

NORTH MACEDONIA 19.06.23

UEFA FOUNDATION

7

THE CAMERA

SON HEUNG-MIN

		MY RATING
ICONIC RATING	★★★☆☆	
DIFFICULTY RATING	★★★★☆	/10
STYLE RATING	★★★☆☆	
FUN RATING	★☆☆☆☆	

6

THE SNIPER

5 PHIL FODEN

ICONIC RATING	★★★★★
DIFFICULTY RATING	★★★★★
STYLE RATING	★★★★★
FUN RATING	★★★★★

MY RATING /10

THE SKY POINT

4 LIONEL MESSI

ICONIC RATING	★★★★★
DIFFICULTY RATING	★★★★★
STYLE RATING	★★★★★
FUN RATING	★★★★★

MY RATING /10

3

Mbappe's brother first did this cele after beating him on FIFA!

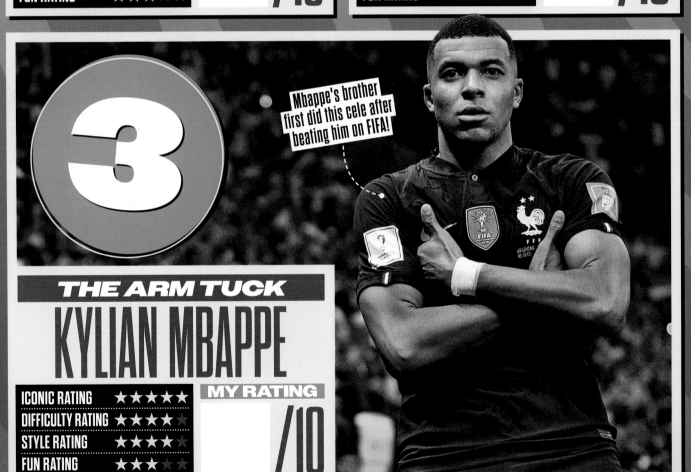

THE ARM TUCK

KYLIAN MBAPPE

ICONIC RATING	★★★★★
DIFFICULTY RATING	★★★★★
STYLE RATING	★★★★★
FUN RATING	★★★★★

MY RATING /10

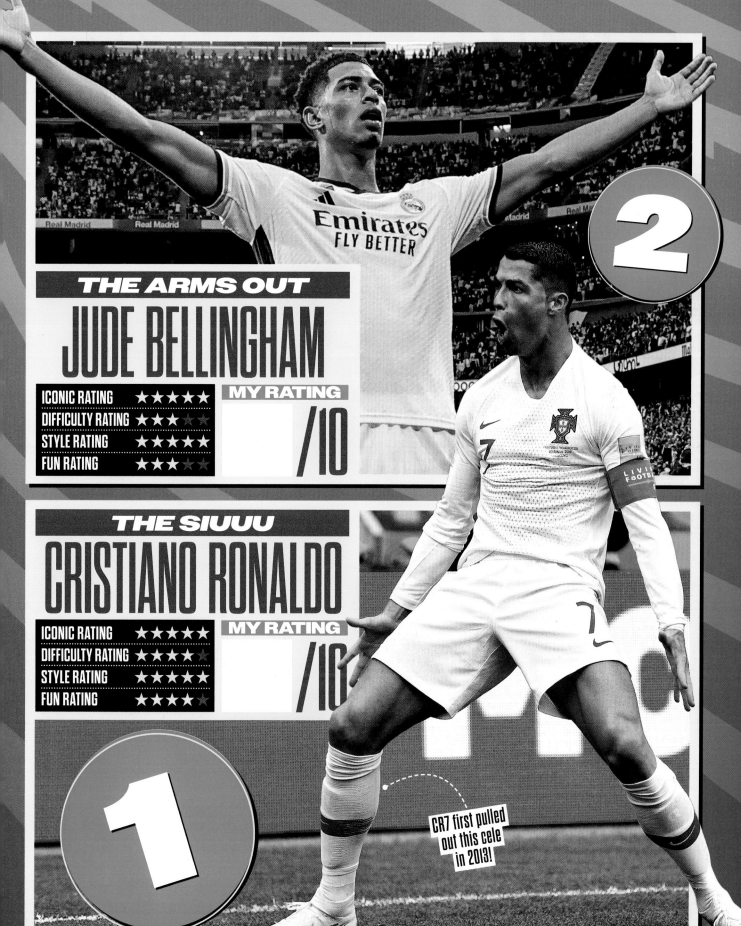

THE ARMS OUT
JUDE BELLINGHAM

ICONIC RATING	★★★★★
DIFFICULTY RATING	★★★☆☆
STYLE RATING	★★★★★
FUN RATING	★★★☆☆

MY RATING /10

2

THE SIUUU
CRISTIANO RONALDO

ICONIC RATING	★★★★★
DIFFICULTY RATING	★★★★☆
STYLE RATING	★★★★★
FUN RATING	★★★★☆

MY RATING /10

1

CR7 first pulled out this cele in 2013!

CRISTIANO RONALDO QUIZ!

IN 2025, Cristiano Ronaldo turns 40! To celebrate his landmark birthday, we are putting your CR7 knowledge to the test!

1 On which island was Cristiano born?

A Majorca
B Lanzarote
C Madeira

2 What's his full name?

A Cristiano Ronaldo Pepe Teixeira
B Cristiano Ronaldo dos Santos Aveiro
C Cristiano Ronaldo Eusebio Campos

3 With which club did he make his debut?

A Sporting Lisbon
B Porto
C Benfica

4 How much did he join Man. United for in 2003?

A £2m
B £12m
C £22m

5 Which Italian club did he play for between 2018 and 2021?

A AC Milan
B Inter Milan
C Juventus

6 How many Champions League titles has he won?

A 3
B 5
C 7

7 Which international tournament did he win with Portugal?

A Euro 2012 ☑
B World Cup 2014 ☑
C Euro 2016 ☑

8 How many times has he won the Ballon d'Or?

A 5 ☑
B 6 ☑
C 7 ☑

9 Who was Man. United manager when Ronaldo rejoined in 2021?

A Jose Mourinho ☑
B Ole Gunnar Solskjaer ☑
C Erik ten Hag ☑

10 Which Saudi Pro League team did he join in January 2023?

A Al-Ittihad ☑
B Al-Ahli ☑
C Al Nassr ☑

ANSWERS ON PAGE 92!

BEARDED BALLERS!

WE IMAGINE HOW SOME OF THE GAME'S BIGGEST SUPERSTARS WOULD LOOK WITH A FACE FULL OF FLUFF!

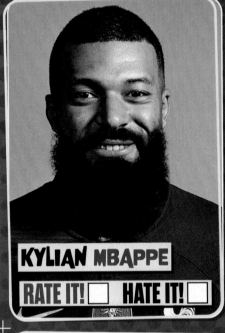

KYLIAN MBAPPE
RATE IT! ☐ HATE IT! ☐

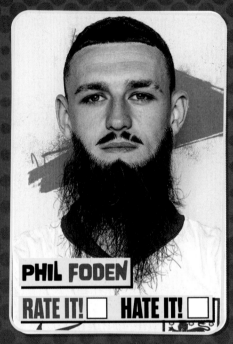

PHIL FODEN
RATE IT! ☐ HATE IT! ☐

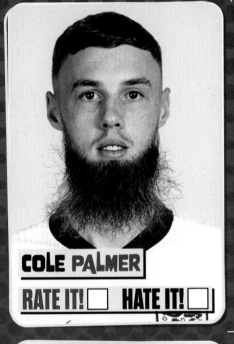

COLE PALMER
RATE IT! ☐ HATE IT! ☐

CRISTIANO RONALDO
RATE IT! ☐ HATE IT! ☐

HARRY KANE
RATE IT! ☐ HATE IT! ☐

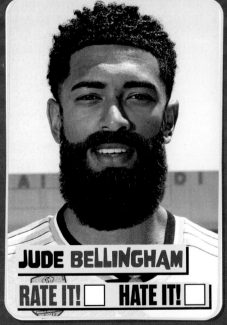

JUDE BELLINGHAM
RATE IT! ☐ HATE IT! ☐

ZINEDINE
ZIDANE

Zizou

1994-2006 | 108 CAPS | 31 GOALS

FRANCE

NO. **10** *Icon*

THE ULTIMATE GUIDE TO...
WOMEN'S FOOTY!

THE WOMEN'S GAME is growing and growing. Get up to speed with this easy MOTD guide!

PART 1
ENGLAND

THE STATS!

ENGLAND ARE THE CURRENT EUROPEAN CHAMPS!
In 2022, the Lionesses beat Germany at Wembley with an epic extra-time goal by Chloe Kelly!

52
England's all-time topscorer is ELLEN WHITE — she netted 52 goals!

SARINA WIEGMAN is the boss and England's most successful coach ever!

The next tournament for the Lionesses is Euro 2025 in Switzerland!

69 MPH

The speed of CHLOE KELLY'S penalty in the 2023 World Cup — faster than any penalty in the Premier League that year!

20:0

The Lionesses' biggest victory was against Latvia in 2021!

152 England's most capped player — man or woman— is FARA WILLIAMS!

THE TEAM!

EARPS

BRIGHT WILLIAMSON

BRONZE CARTER

WALSH

STANWAY TOONE

MEAD HEMP

RUSSO

THE PLAYERS!

MARY EARPS
Club: PSG

LUCY BRONZE
Club: Chelsea

MILLIE BRIGHT
Club: Chelsea

LEAH WILLIAMSON
Club: Arsenal

JESS CARTER
Club: Gotham FC

GEORGIA STANWAY
Club: Bayern Munich

KEIRA WALSH
Club: Barcelona

ELLA TOONE
Club: Man. United

LAUREN HEMP
Club: Man. City

BETH MEAD
Club: Arsenal

ALESSIA RUSSO
Club: Arsenal

PART 2

THE WSL

The WSL is the top tier of women's football in England!

THE GOALSCORERS!

Keep your eyes on **KHADIJA SHAW**. The Jamaica star won the Golden Boot in 2023-24, netting 21 goals!

The best for banging in headers is Tottenham striker **BETHANY ENGLAND** — she scored 17 last season!

Want an assist? Look for **LAUREN HEMP**. The speedy Man. City star clocked up eight assists last season!

THE CLUBS!

There are 12 teams in the WSL. This season, **CRYSTAL PALACE WOMEN** are playing in the WSL for the first time ever!

THE FANS!

1 MILLION

fans attended a WSL or Women's Championship game in 2023-24!

7

Chelsea are the current champions. The Blues have won the league seven times and now they're trying for their sixth League title in a row!

THE SHOT STOPPER!

KHIARA KEATING became the youngest-ever player to win the Golden Glove in 2023-24. Khiara kept nine clean sheets!

9

PART 3
THE WOMEN'S UCL

THE TOURNAMENT!

The 2025 final will be held in LISBON!

16
teams play in the group stages!

THE WINNERS!

BARCELONA are the current champs — they've played in the last four UCL finals!

THE GOALSCORER!

KADIDIATOU DIANI is last season's UCL top goalscorer — she netted eight goals!

8
LYON ARE UCL history-makers. No club has collected more UCL trophies than the French club!

UCL TROPHY WINNERS

8 Lyon
4 Frankfurt
3 Barcelona

THE SUPERSTAR!

Barcelona baller AITANA BONMATI is the best women's player on the planet. She was the UCL Player of the tournament and UCL Player of the Match last year!

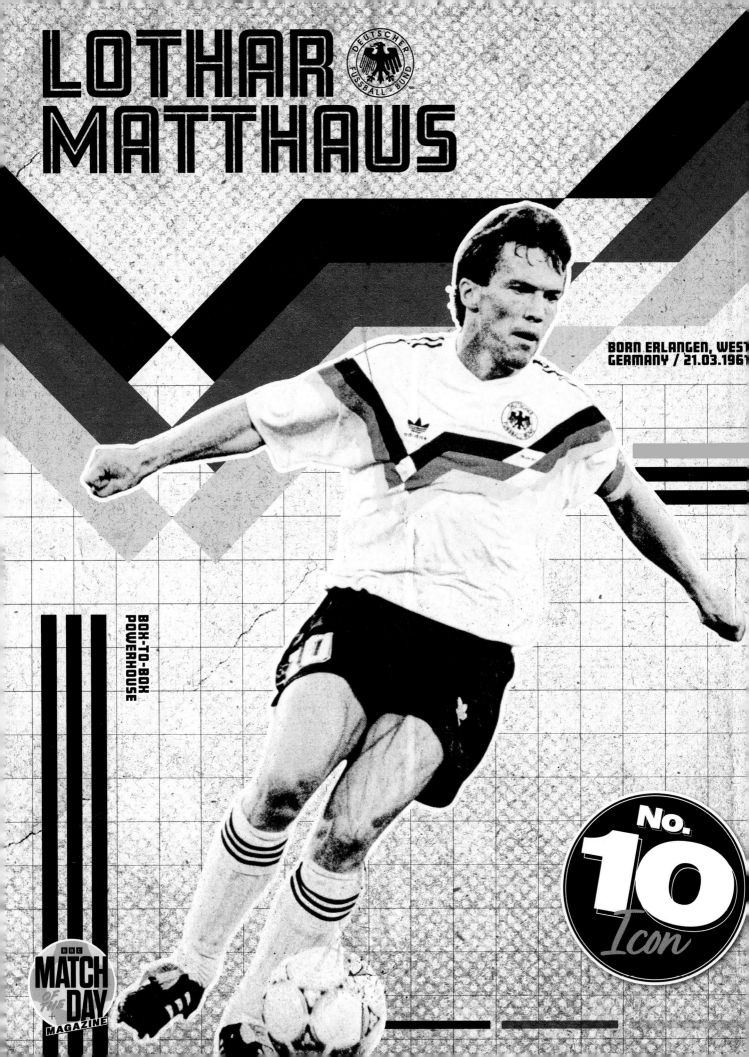

LOTHAR MATTHAUS

BORN ERLANGEN, WEST GERMANY / 21.03.1961

BOX-TO-BOX POWERHOUSE

No. 10 Icon

MATCH OF THE DAY MAGAZINE

Ruud Gullit

Totaalvoetbal

Netherlands

1987 Ballon d'Or
winner

No.
10
Icon

THE BEST OF THE BEST!

It's time to celebrate everything amazing about the greatest sport on the planet!

THE BEST GOAL TO SCORE...

BICYCLE KICK

The best goals are the ones that you couldn't recreate with 100 more tries! That's why bicycle kicks are the best of all. Getting your mate to swing in a whippy cross that you have to fire home from in the air behind you? It's a one-in-a-million goal!

MY PICK! ....

40

GUNNERSAURUS

■ The ledge green dinosaur is everyone's bessie mate at the Emirates! On matchdays, Gunner doesn't walk two steps without busting a move, grabbing selfies with fans or hyping up the Arsenal stars. Simply put, this dino dude is a footy icon!

Who's your favourite mascot?

MY PICK! ....

THE BEST OF ALL TIME...

LIONEL MESSI

■ The Argentina icon has magic in his boots and more tek than any player ever before! That's why Leo is our GOAT. In his prime, his dribbling was genuinely unstoppable and his ability to score worldies and play perfect passes was unmatched!

MY PICK! ....

ALEXIA PUTELLAS

■ Lex is an all-time legend! The mega tekky midfielder has inspired both Barcelona and Spain to lifting countless trophies, thanks to her ability to bag assists and dominate matches. She can dribble, shoot and works super hard to keep her team on top!

MY PICK!

RAINBOW FLICK

Can you do the rainbow flick?

■ It's the ultimate humiliation! Flicking the ball up over your head — and a defender! It will get the crowd up off their seats, but it's well hard to get right. Brazilian ballers like Neymar and Vinicius Jr have mastered this skill — have you?

MY PICK! ....

CHAMPIONS LEAGUE

There's little better than big ears, here! The Champions League trophy is truly iconic. It's the trophy that young ballers fall asleep and dream about winning. Even the biggest stars in the game get excited about lifting it!

MY PICK! ....

KYLIAN MBAPPE

Do you think King Kyl is the best player in the world?

This flames forward is the deadliest baller on planet Earth! France's Kyl is a goal machine who uses all his pace and agility to tie defenders in knots. After he's done all that, Mbappe's got the finishing and passing tek to change games!

MY PICK!

THE BEST BADGE...

KOLN

There are so many sick badges in football, that it's almost impossible to pick the best of all. There are historic ones like AC Milan and weird-shaped ones like Corinthians, but we have so much love for this well silly goat one from German second-tier club Koln!

MY PICK! ....

THE BEST WONDERKID...

LAMINE YAMAL

Barcelona have the two best young players in the world! Forward Salma Paralluelo is a firework for their women's team — but this 17-year-old is already a game-changing talent as we saw at the Euros. Yamal could rule footy for the next decade!

MY PICK! ....

Antoine Griezmann was a World Cup winner in 2018!

THE BEST TOURNAMENT...

WORLD CUP

The World Cup is the pinnacle of football! Every four years we get a men's and a women's World Cup where all of the game's top players compete for glory. It creates the best footy and atmosphere on the planet!

MY PICK! ....

THE BEST KIT...

BRAZIL

There isn't a more iconic kit than Brazil's samba-styled, yellow and green home strip with blue shorts. Every time we see this kit, we think of sunshine, dancing and vibey, tekky, skilful players using all their tricks to set games on fire!

MY PICK! ....

THE BEST HAIRCUT...

ERLING HAALAND

Erling might well be the best goalscorer in world footy, but we reckon he's definitely the best hair grower. The long blonde locks really work for the big Norwegian, creating a trademark look that tons of fans try to copy!

MY PICK! ....

Is there a better boot than the Predator?

THE BEST BOOTS...

ADIDAS PREDATOR

Preds are classics! Back in the day, football heroes like Zinedine Zidane and David Beckham wore these boots, but these days modern icons like Jude Bellingham and Alessia Russo trust them on their feet. It helps that they always look absolutely stunning!

MY PICK! ....

THE BEST STADIUM...

LA BOMBONERA

■ This is a stadium unlike any you've ever been to! It's got an amazing design, all splashed in the classy blue and yellow colourway of Argentinian giants Boca Juniors. More importantly though, the atmosphere inside it is truly one of a kind!

MY PICK! ....

THE BEST PLAYGROUND GAME...

HEADERS AND VOLLEYS

■ Got a group of mates and a ball? Then there's no better game to play than this! The keeper counts to 60 while you try to head or volley the ball past them. The scenes when the countdown gets into the last few seconds are always epic!

MY PICK! ....

THE BEST MANAGER...

PEP GUARDIOLA

Pep's won 38 trophies in 15 seasons as a manager!

■ Pep is a footy genius! The Man. City manager has won every trophy possible in club football, thanks to his top tactical knowledge and perfect player management. He's the master of building unstoppable football teams!

MY PICK! ....

THE BEST TIFO...

PSG YODA

■ Tifos are massive flags or banners that mega fans make to hype up their team before matches! There have been so many amazing ones over the years, but our current fave is this one from the PSG fans. It's of Star Wars OG Yoda — how bantz!

MY PICK! ....

THE BEST BALL...

CHAMPIONS LEAGUE BALL

■ Each year the Champions League ball steps up and stands out! It's got that elite starry design that gets remixed each season, which we're convinced helps you play better. Playing with it makes every game a special one!

MY PICK! ....

Are you Team Messi or Team Ronaldo?

THE BEST RIVALRY EVER...

RONALDO v MESSI

■ The battles Cristiano Ronaldo and Lionel Messi have had — to win trophies and become the best player to ever exist — were so entertaining to watch. CR7 has more Champions League titles, but Messi boasts more Ballons d'Or. Who's your GOAT?

MY PICK! ....

INTER MILAN
SERIE A CHAMPIONS

2023-24

LE
WIN

CELTIC
SPFL
CHAMPIONS

BAYER LEVERKUSEN
BUNDESLIGA CHAMPIONS

CHELSEA
WSL CHAMPIONS

AGUE
NERS

MAN. CITY
PREMIER LEAGUE CHAMPIONS

PSG
LIGUE 1 CHAMPIONS

REAL MADRID
LA LIGA CHAMPIONS

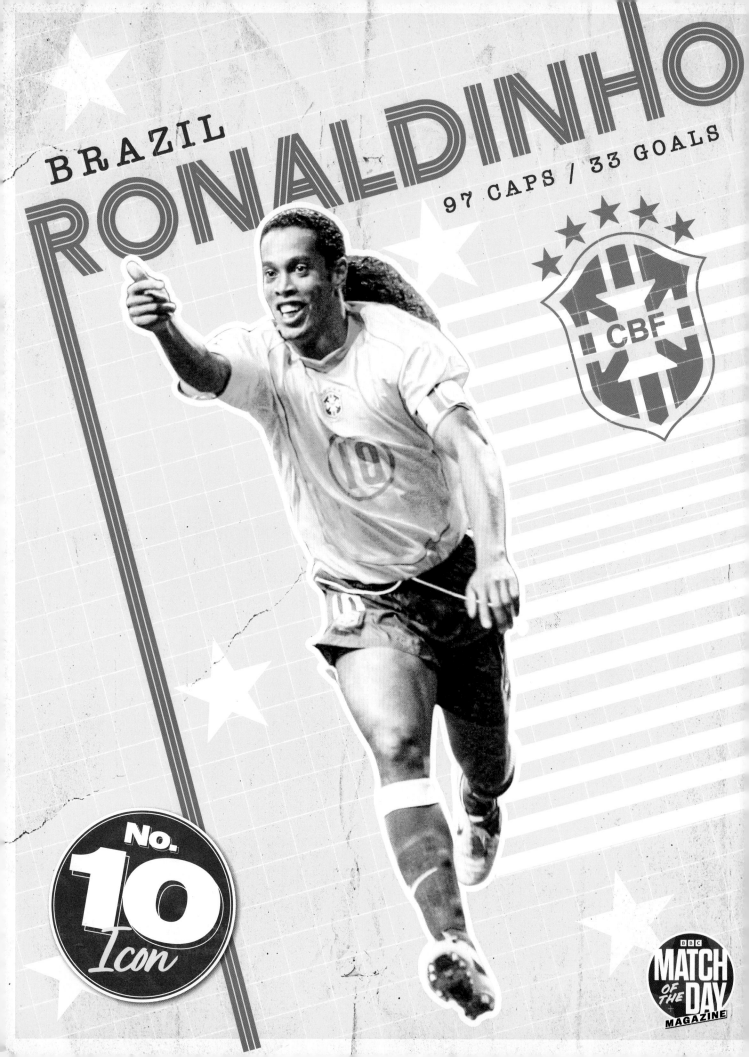

EURO 2024

THE PHOTO ALBUM! 📷

MOTD celebrates the summer of superstar ballers, spicy goals and sick saves! Turn over for the biggest and best tournament photo dump!

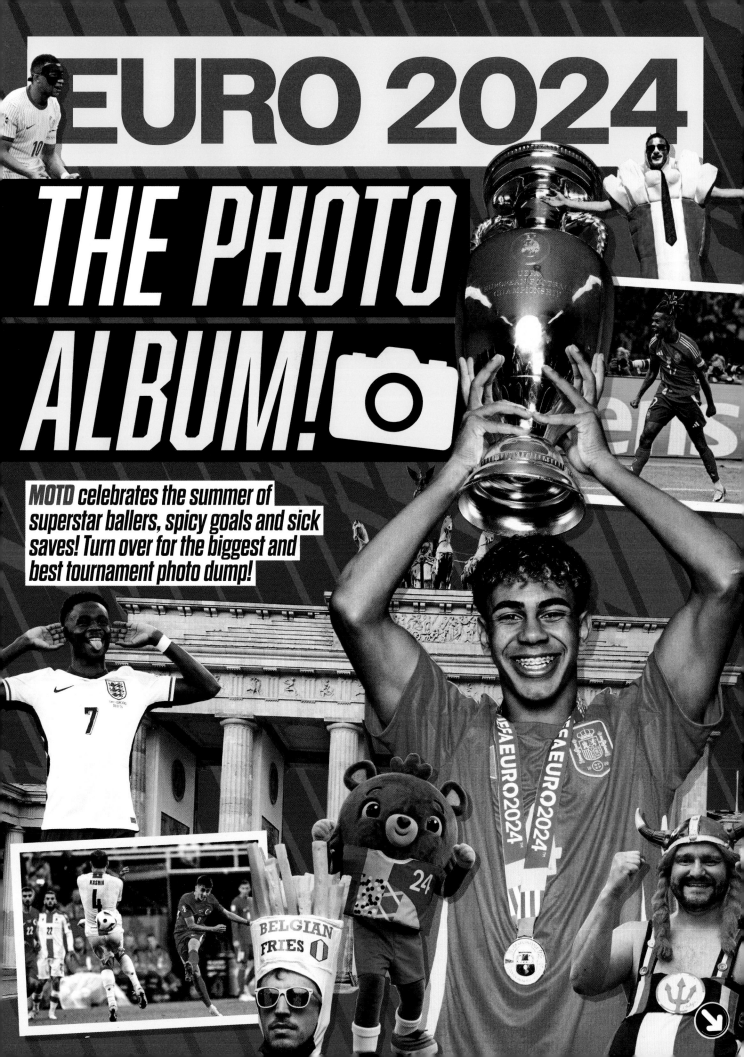

THE BALLERS!

KING KANE!

■ Harry Kane did it again. The England captain became the Euros all-time top scorer in the knockout stages and shared the Golden Boot!

TEEN SUPERSTAR!

■ Lamine Yamal was the star of the show. The 16-year-old became the youngest player to score at a Euros — fizzing in an epic goal against France!

RAPID WINGERS!

■ No-one could catch Germany's Jamal Musiala and Spain's Nico Williams — these two wicked wingers sent defenders spinning!

GALACTICO GULER!

■ Nineteen-year-old Arda Guler announced himself in some style, too. His ace goal from outside the box against Georgia transformed him into a national treasure in Turkey!

EPIC 'OLDIES'!

■ N'Golo Kante was cooking! The France midfielder was back to his brilliant best — he won two Player of the Match awards!

■ At 41, Pepe became the oldest player to feature at any Euros tournament — the Portugal defender was on fire!

MASKED MBAPPE!

■ Kylian Mbappe's face mask became iconic — it was more talked about than France's football!

RECORD-BUSTING RONNIE!

■ It was a record-breaking sixth Euros for CR7. But the Portugal ledge couldn't top up his tally of 14 tournament goals — despite 23 attempts — only Mbappe had more!

UNLUCKY LUKAKU!

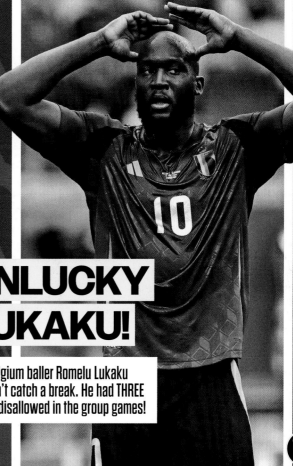

■ Belgium baller Romelu Lukaku couldn't catch a break. He had THREE goals disallowed in the group games!

THE GOALS!

There were 117 goals in the tournament! Here are just some of MOTD's most memorable...

ZINGERS!

■ Romania's captain Nicolae Stanciu curled a cracker into the top corner in their opening game against Ukraine!

SPEEDY GOALS!

■ Blink and you'd miss Albania's Nedim Bajrami. He netted against Italy in just 23 seconds — the fastest in Euros history!

OWN GOALS!

■ There were ten own goals in the tournament. Antonio Rudiger gave Scotland fans something to celebrate — the Germany star headed into his own net in the opening game. Oops!

A NO-LOOK GOAL!

■ In England's quarter-final shootout against Switzerland, Ivan Toney's ice-cold pen became iconic. He stared down Yann Sommer, shot and scored — he didn't even look at the ball!

LATE GOALS!

■ The Euros had all the epic last-gasp goals. Ollie Watkins fired England into the semis with this unforgettable 90th-min winner. Just look at his face!

MAGIC GOALS!

■ England needed a superhero to save them against Slovakia. They had one: Jude Bellingham scored a brilliant bicycle kick in the 95th minute! Who else?

THE SAVES!

It was all action in between the sticks too!

LAST-MINUTE LEAP!

■ Turkey keeper Mert Gunok sprung to save from Austria's Christoph Baumgartner in the last minute!

PICKFORD'S CHEAT SHEET!

■ Always do your homework! Jordan Pickford prepped all of Switzerland's penalty moves and stuck them onto his water bottle. Pickford saved — and England won!

STICKS SUPERHERO!

■ Portugal's Diogo Costa became the first keeper in Euros history to save three pens in one shootout!

THE FANS!

Euro 2024 was a festival for the fans!

German sax player Andre Schnura played the tunes...

The Tartan Army brought the vibes...

The Dutch fans bounced...

Others roared...

...and this fan snored!

THE MAD MOMENTS!

There were some weird and wonderful moments too...

DANCING DANES!

■ These dancing Danish fans didn't mind getting a drenching!

STORMY STADIUMS!

■ The weather was as electric as the action. An epic thunderstorm postponed play at the BVB Stadion in Dortmund!

THE HAIR-LIGHTS!

■ Robert Andrich disguised himself as a pink highlighter pen and Romania's Andrei Ratiu rocked a 'Smurf blue' do!

THE FOOD FIGHTS!

BELGIAN FRIES ♥ BETTER THAN FRENCH FRIES

BELGIAN FRIES

■ Fans faced off with funny food fight signs...

■ ...or dressed as their national dish!

THE WINNERS!

SIZZLING SPAIN!

■ Spain were the winners and the team of the tournament — slaying Italy, Croatia, Germany, France and England on the way. They are the only team to win all their games in a tournament since Brazil in 2002. The trophy is the country's fourth European championship title — no other nation has won more!

INDIVIDUAL AWARDS!

PLAYER OF THE TOURNAMENT

■ Rodri, Spain

GOLDEN BOOT

■ The prize was shared between six players with three goals each:

- Cody Gakpo, Netherlands
- Harry Kane, England
- Georges Mikautadze, Georgia
- Jamal Musiala, Germany
- Dani Olmo, Spain
- Ivan Schranz, Slovakia

YOUNG PLAYER OF THE TOURNAMENT

■ Lamine Yamal, Spain

GOLDEN GLOVE

■ Mike Maignan, France

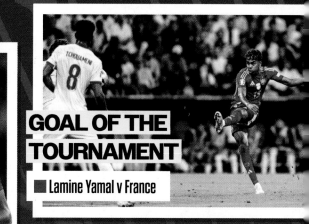

GOAL OF THE TOURNAMENT

■ Lamine Yamal v France

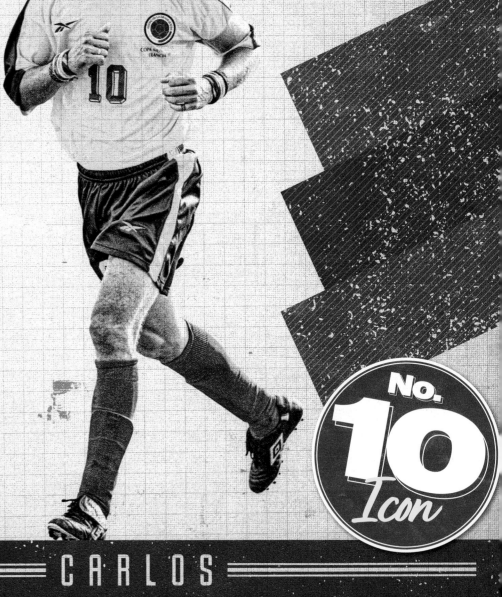

No. 10 Icon

C A R L O S

VALDERRAMA

COLOMBIA

GUESS WHO?

Adam? Never heard of him!

Can you guess the HIDDEN BALLERS in the photos?

1

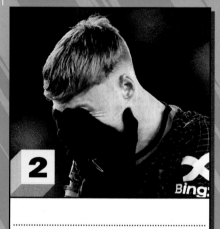
2

3

4

5

6

7

8

9

YOUR FOOTY BRAIN POWER

9	GENIUS
7	PROFESSIONAL
5	SEMI-PRO
3	AMATEUR
1	SUNDAY LEAGUE
0	OH NO, DISASTER

YOUR SCORE ☐ /9

ANSWERS ON PAGE 92!

25 FOOTY THINGS TO DO IN 2025!

How many of these **25 footy challenges** can YOU crush in 2025?

CHALLENGE SECTIONS

1 FOOTY TEK!

2 SUPERFAN!

3 CREATIVE KING!

4 FOOTY BRAIN!

SECTION 1: FOOTY TEK!

1 CRUSH 25 KEEPY-UPPIES!

Do 25 keepy-uppies — and save a special move for the 25th!

COMPLETED IT! ✓

2 BE A HAT-TRICK HERO!

Score three goals in a game — the perfect hat-trick is one right-footed goal, one left-footed AND a header!

COMPLETED IT! ✓

3 SUPERCHARGE YOUR SPRINTS!

Put on a T-shirt over the top of your own and ask your friend to hold the bottom of it. Start running towards a target — see if you can speed away from your friend to get there!

MOTD SAYS...
Use an old T-shirt — don't rip a new one!

COMPLETED IT! ✓

4 START A CELEBRATION!

Team up with your mates and make up a new season cele!

COMPLETED IT! ✓

5 PRACTISE 25 PENS!

Most players strike the same pens — mix them up with different run-ups, different targets, and by connecting with the ball using different levels of power!

COMPLETED IT! ✓

6 BOSS THE BICYCLE KICK!

Grab some mates and recreate Alejandro Garnacho's goal of the season!

COMPLETED IT! ✓

7 BE AN ALL-SURFACE STAR!

Don't just play on grass — try your footy skills on different surfaces and in different spaces. Whether it's a sandy beach to inside a cage — just be sure it's safe!

COMPLETED IT! ✓

8 LOB THE KEEPER!

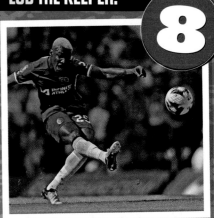

Catch the keeper off their line, look up and lob them from outside the area!

COMPLETED IT! ✓

25 CHALLENGES
SECTION 2: SUPER FAN!

9

COMPLETED IT! ✔

10 FIND SOME FOOTY WALL ART!

DESIGN A MURAL
Draw a mural that brightens up this bare wall.
Plan a design that celebrates your favourite club
or favourite player's most memorable moment!

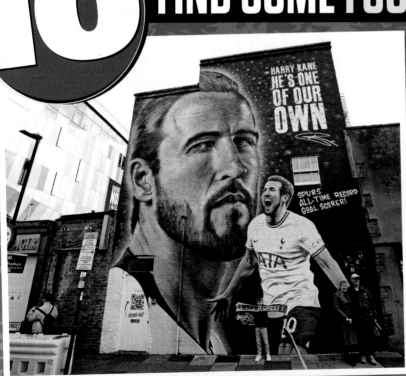

HARRY KANE
HE'S ONE
OF OUR
OWN

SPURS'
ALL-TIME RECORD
GOAL SCORER!

COMPLETED IT! ✔

SPOT A SUPERSTAR STATUE!

This is the Thierry Henry statue at Arsenal's Emirates Stadium!

11

COMPLETED IT! ✓

12

GET A PIC WITH A PLAYER!

Which baller would YOU like a photo with?

STAR SELFIE
Which star would YOU most like a selfie with? Draw you and your selfie star here!

COMPLETED IT!

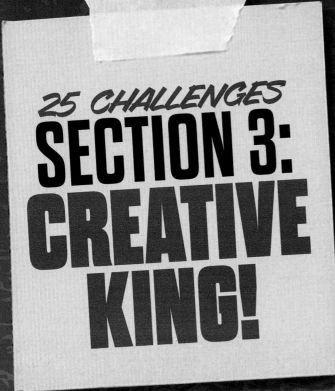

25 CHALLENGES

SECTION 3: CREATIVE KING!

BUILD A STADIUM!

Start saving old shoe and cereal boxes, toilet rolls and tinfoil – because it's time to craft an epic replica of your fave footy stadium. Don't forget the pitch, the floodlights and the fans!

MOTD SAYS... Check with an adult before you start!

13

COMPLETED IT! ✔

14

CUSTOMISE YOUR KICKS!

Take some fabric pens, thread some colourful new laces and personalise your boots – they'll pop on the pitch!

MOTD SAYS... Check with an adult and plan your design first!

SOME IDEAS TO TRY:
- Add your initials
- Add your signature
- Add your club's badge
- Add your country's crest
- Add a positive footy phrase

COMPLETED IT! ✔

START A SEASON SCRAPBOOK!

15

Fill a scrapbook with your favourite footy memories for this season. Stick in tickets, photos, stickers and add your own match reports!

COMPLETED IT! ✔

DESIGN A KIT!

16

Give your fave team a fresh new 'fit for 2025! Draw a new design and add some brand-new tech for 2025, too. How about a torch, 'anti-pull' material or built-in water and energy gels?

COMPLETED IT!

REDESIGN YOUR CLUB BADGE!

17

Give your favourite club's badge a new design for 2025!

COMPLETED IT! ✔

WRITE A CHANT!

WRITE A CHANT OR SONG FOR YOUR FAVOURITE NEW PLAYER!

18

Write the name, nickname, skill, hometown of that player and think of rhyming words!

COMPLETED IT!

25 CHALLENGES
SECTION 4: FOOTY BRAIN!

19

BE A BADGE BOSS!

Learn and name the 20 Premier League club badges!

COMPLETED IT! ✓

20

LEARN ABOUT A LEDGE!

Go back 25 years in footy time and find out about the top talents from the 2000s. Find out their nickname, their story and their super skill!

LUIS FIGO
Nickname:
Country:
Position:
Superstar skill:

ZINEDINE ZIDANE
Nickname:
Country:
Position:
Superstar skill:

DAVID BECKHAM
Nickname:
Country:
Position:
Superstar skill:

COMPLETED IT! ✓

GET STADIUM SAVVY!

Learn the names of the 20 stadiums in the Premier League!

21

Which stadium is...

the closest to where you live?

the oldest?

the biggest?

your favourite?

COMPLETED IT! ✓

GET SUPERSCORER SMART!

22

Make it your mission to find out who the top scorer is for:

Your club: _____

Your country: _____

COMPLETED IT! ✓

SPEAK FOOTBALL!

Find out how to say 'football' in these four Euro languages!

 *FRENCH:*
_____

 *GERMAN:*
_____

 *ITALIAN:*
_____

 *SPANISH:*
_____

COMPLETED IT! ✓

24

TRY COMMENTATING!

Watch two mins of highlights on Match of the Day on BBC iPlayer — but turn the sound off. Try to describe a goal. Then, rewind the footage and compare your description to the commentator's!

COMPLETED IT! ✓

MASTER THE MASCOTS!

25

Learn the names of the mascots for the 20 different clubs in the Prem!

Which one is YOUR fave? _____

COMPLETED IT! ✓

TOT UP YOUR TOTALS!
HOW MANY DID YOU COMPLETE?

I COMPLETED ...... /25 CHALLENGES

RUI COSTA

THE MAESTRO
1993–2004

94 CAPS
26 GOALS

PORTUGAL

No.
10
Icon

ROBERTO

BAGGIO

**Il Divin Codino
/ The Divine
Ponytail**

ITALY

Michael
Laudrup
DANISH DYNAMITE

Denmark

NO.
10
Icon

QUIZ AN ADULT!

It's time to see just how much your chosen adult knows about football. Are they a genuine footy brainiac or when it matters, will they crumble under the pressure? LET'S FIND OUT!

BEFORE YOU START!

YOUR ADULT WILL NEED...

✓ A CUP OF TEA (MAYBE EVEN A BISCUIT OR TWO)

✓ THEIR FAVE SLIPPERS

✓ A PEN

YOU ARE THE QUIZ MASTER!

NO CHEETAHS or CHEATERS ALLOWED!

QUIZ AN ADULT!

1 NAME THESE TWO STARS WHO JOINED NORTH LONDON SIDE ARSENAL IN 1997!

PLAYER A

PLAYER B

2 WHICH CLUB HAS NEVER PLAYED IN THE PREMIER LEAGUE?

| A Barnsley ✓ | B Swindon ✓ | C Portsmouth ✓ | D Millwall ✓ |

3 NAME THESE TWO PFA AWARD WINNERS FROM 1993!

PLAYER A

PLAYER B

4 WHICH PREM CLUBS WORE THESE ICONIC SHIRTS BACK IN THE '90s?

A ....

B ....

C ....

5 WHICH PREMIER LEAGUE CLUB DID THESE FOUR MEN MANAGE?

....

6 DID THESE STRIKERS EVER WIN THE PREMIER LEAGUE GOLDEN BOOT?

A Kevin Phillips ☑ YES ☑ NO

B Robbie Fowler ☑ YES ☑ NO

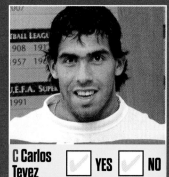

C Carlos Tevez ☑ YES ☑ NO

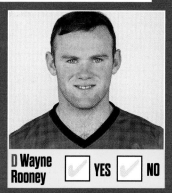

D Wayne Rooney ☑ YES ☑ NO

ANSWERS ON PAGE 92!

8 WHAT'S THE NAME OF THIS FORMER LIVERPOOL MIDFIELDER?

....

9 NWANKWO KANU SCORED THE WINNER FOR WHO IN THE 2008 FA CUP FINAL?

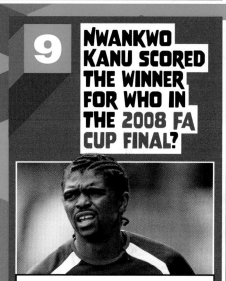

....

10 NAME THESE TWO ENGLAND INTERNATIONALS DOWN UNDER IN 1991!

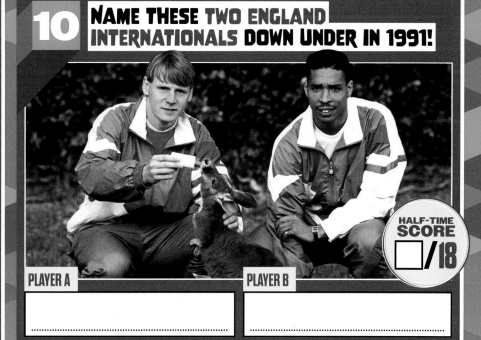

PLAYER A

....

PLAYER B

....

HALF-TIME SCORE ☐ /18

7 WHO IS THIS PREMIER LEAGUE STAR OF THE 1990s?

....

QUIZ AN ADULT!

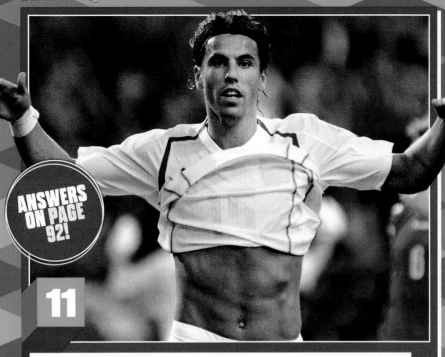

ANSWERS ON PAGE 92!

11

THIS CZECH REPUBLIC STAR WAS TOP SCORER AT EURO 2004 IN PORTUGAL – WHO IS IT?

- A Jan Koller
- B Savo Milosevic
- C Milan Baros
- D Nuno Gomes

12

WHO DID LIVERPOOL BEAT IN THE 2005 CHAMPIONS LEAGUE FINAL?

- A Real Madrid
- B AC Milan
- C Barcelona
- D Juventus

13

HE SCORED THE WINNER IN THE EURO 96 FINAL – WHAT'S HIS NAME?

- A Thomas Hassler
- B Matthias Sammer
- C Oliver Bierhoff
- D Thomas Strunz

14

WHAT IS THE NAME OF THIS ICONIC WORLD CUP MASCOT?

- A Juanito
- B Pepo
- C Som Brero
- D Pique

15

WHICH OF THESE PLAYERS DID NOT SCORE AT EURO 2004?

A Frank Lampard

B Paul Scholes

C Steven Gerrard

D David Beckham

16 WHO DID SPAIN BEAT 4-0 IN THE EURO 2012 FINAL?

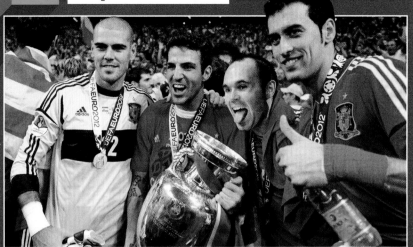

A Croatia	B Germany
C Italy	D Netherlands

17 WHICH COUNTRY WON THE 2002 WORLD CUP?

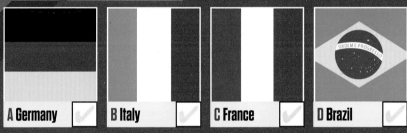

A Germany	B Italy	C France	D Brazil

18

WHO MANAGED ENGLAND AT THE 2010 WORLD CUP?

A Sven-Goran Eriksson	B Steve McClaren
C Fabio Capello	D Roy Hodgson

19 WHO WON THE FIRST CHAMPIONS LEAGUE IN 1993?

A AC Milan B Ajax

C Marseille D Real Madrid

20 WHO WON THE 1998 WORLD CUP GOLDEN BOOT?

A Davor Suker B Ronaldo

C Zinedine Zidane D Gabriel Batistuta

How did you do?

FULL-TIME SCORE /28

77

CAN YOU WIN THE PREMIER LEAGUE?

CAN YOU steer your squad to become Premier League champions? Grab a dice and some mates, then play the game!

23

24 You get stuck behind a tractor on the way to play Ipswich! MOVE BACK 2

25 **26**

27 Warm-weather training! MOVE FORWARD 3

22

48 It's the final matchday and your fans bring all the good vibes! MOVE FORWARD 1

49 FINISH

21 NEW BOOTS BOOST! THROW AGAIN!

47

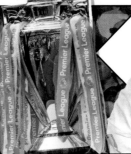

20

46

45 Your mascot gets overexcited and goes onto the pitch! He's banned! MOVE BACK 4

44 **43** **42** **4**

19 Over Christmas, your keeper eats too much Xmas pud! MISS A TURN

18

VAR ROLL THE DICE! **17**

16 A Saudi team tempts your best player with a mega-money deal! MOVE BACK 8

HOW TO PLAY

- Each player chooses a manager. Ask a grown-up to help you carefully cut out the managers with the scissors.
- Place the counters on the start.
- Take turns to roll the dice. Move the number of spaces as shown on the dice. If a player lands on a space with an instruction, do as it says.
- If you land on a VAR card — roll the dice again. If you throw 4-6 move forward that number of spaces. If you throw 1-3 move back that number of spaces.
- If you land on a BOOTS boost — throw the dice again.
- The winner is the first player to arrive at the trophy!

THE MANAGERS

GUARDIOLA **SLOT** **ARTETA** **ADAM**

START

1

2

3
Uh-oh! Your new stadium isn't ready!
MOVE BACK 2

4

8

29

30

Your captain scores a last-minute own goal!
MOVE BACK 5

31

32

VAR
ROLL THE DICE!
33

5

34

6

NEW BOOTS BOOST!
THROW AGAIN!

35

7

36
Your forwards fight over who takes the pens!
MISS A TURN

VAR
ROLL THE DICE!
40

39

38

NEW BOOTS BOOST!
THROW AGAIN!

37

8
Your striker bags a hat-trick in the first home game!
MOVE FORWARD 3

15

14

13

12
Your new 3rd kit is scratchy!
MOVE BACK 2

11

10

9

BUILD THE ULTIMATE ANIMAL 5-A-SIDE TEAM!

THE RULE! Pick ONE animal from each row!

THE BUDGET £200M

Build your own ANIMAL 5-A-SIDE TEAM, sticking to your £200m budget...

GK
- CHIMPANZEE £40M
- POLAR BEAR £30M
- GIANT PANDA £20M
- TAPIR £10M

DF
- GORILLA £40M
- CROCODILE £30M
- HIPPO £20M
- HYENA £10M

CM
- BROWN BEAR £60M
- RHINO £50M
- BISON £40M
- OTTER £30M

FW
- CHEETAH £60M
- EAGLE £50M
- CAMEL £40M
- PENGUIN £30M

ST
- KANGAROO £70M
- LION £60M
- TIGER £50M
- OSTRICH £40M

Gheorghe HAGI

Romania

FEDERATIA ROMANA
*FONDATA IN

The Maradona of
the Carpathians

1983-2000
124 caps

No.
10
Icon

BALLER

PARTY TIME

COLOUR IT IN!

BIRTHDAY!

WHO'S THE BALLER?

The answer to each question is one of the players pictured on this page —good luck!

1 He made his professional debut against Portsmouth!

....

2 He scored the winning goal in the 2021 Champions League final!

....

3 He went to university and has a degree in business administration!

....

4 He could have played international football for African country Burundi!

....

5 He has an international airport named after him!

....

6 He was named Millwall's Young Player of the Year in 2011—12!

ANSWERS ON P92!

....

7 He was on trial at Chelsea when he was 11 years old!

....

MBAPPE

It finally happened! The France captain made his dream move and Madrid got their man.

MANIA!

Here's everything you need to know about Real Madrid's megastar...

MBAPPE *FACTS!*

Name: Kylian Mbappe Lottin
Date of birth: 20 December 1998
Position: Forward
Club: Real Madrid

Mbappe's fam!

■ Kylian comes from a sporty family. His dad is a football coach and his mum was a handball player. His adopted brother, Jires is an ex-footballer and his kid brother, Ethan, plays for Lille!

Mbappe's hometown!

■ Kylian is proud of his hometown of Bondy, a suburb of Paris. It even has huge mural of Mbappe!

Mbappe's speed!

■ Kylian is still one of the fastest footballers on the planet — he's hit top speeds of 23mph!

Mbappe's idols!

■ Mbappe's heroes are two Real Madrid legends: Zinedine Zidane and Cristiano Ronaldo. As a kid, Kylian had posters of CR7 and liked Zidane so much, he even asked a barber to cut his hair like him — with a bald patch in it!

MBAPPE'S MILESTONES! From Bondy to the Bernabeu!

1998

Kylian is born! It's a special year for French football. France win their first World Cup!

Plays for his local club, Bondy. Kylian is so good, he plays against the older boys!

2008

2013

Scouted by Arsenal, Chelsea and Real Madrid. He stays in France and signs for Monaco!

16 de julio de 2024

Mbappe's trophies!

■ Kylian's trophy cabinet is stacked! He's won 17 major trophies including:

1 World Cup

7 Ligue 1 titles

4 French Cups

Mbappe's goals!

■ Kylian's netted 331 goals for club and country, and an incredible 19 career hat-tricks!

What will Mbappe do at Real Madrid?

■ Lift the La Liga title ☑

■ Win the Champions League ☑

■ Win the Ballon d'Or ☑

■ (your idea) ☑

....

....

*Stats correct up to 1 August 2024.

2017

Lifts the Ligue 1 title with Monaco. Scores his first Champions League goal, against Man. City!

2017

Signs for PSG. They win Ligue 1. It's the first of six titles for Kyl at the club!

2018

Plays for France in the 2018 World Cup — and wins it. He's the first teen to score in a World Cup final since Pele!

2022

Scores a hat-trick in an epic World Cup final against Argentina. But France lose on penalties!

2024

Makes his dream move. Mbappe is a Madridista!

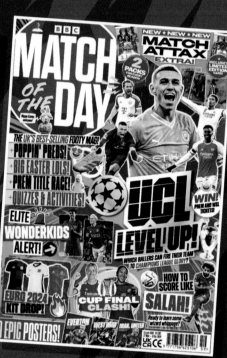

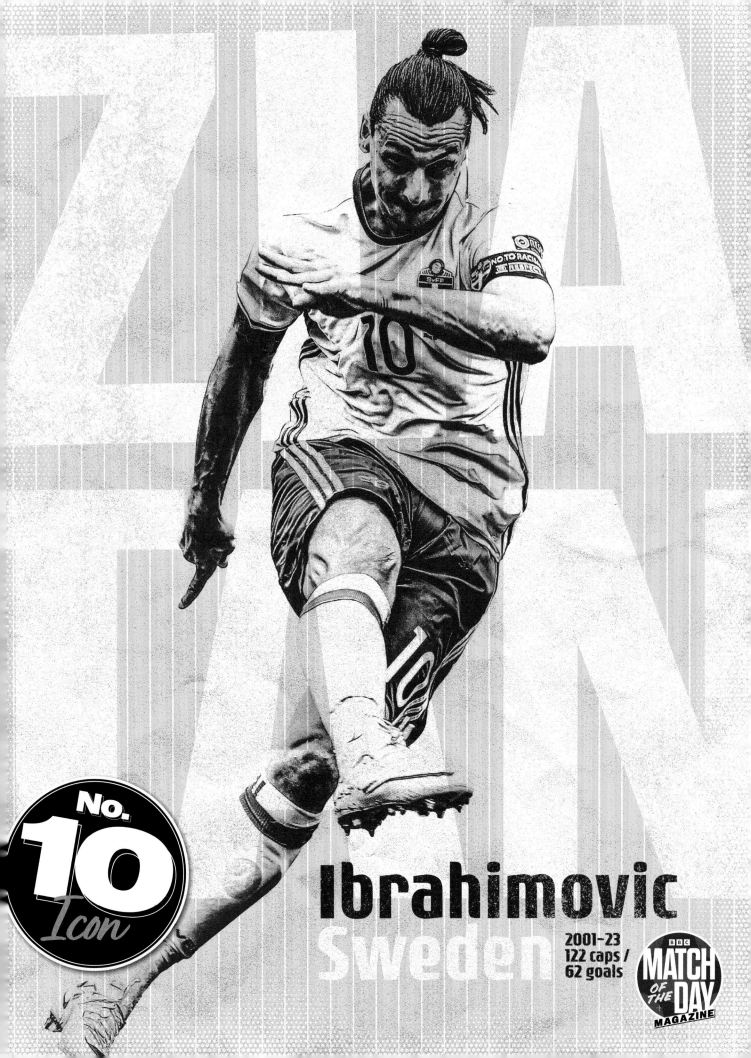

No.
10
Icon

Ibrahimovic
Sweden

2001–23
122 caps /
62 goals

BBC
MATCH
OF
THE
DAY
MAGAZINE

SPOT THE BALL!

We've removed the ball from the FOUR ENGLAND PHOTOS below – can you guess where it should be?

BALL 1

A B C D E F G
1 2 3 4

ANSWER: ....

BALL 2

A B C D E F G
1 2 3 4

ANSWER: ....

BALL 3

A B C D E F G
1 2 3 4

ANSWER: ....

BALL 4

A B C D E F G
1 2 3 4

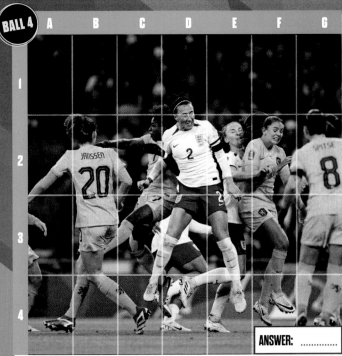

ANSWER: ....

WSL CLUBS WORDSEARCH!

Can you find all 12 WSL CLUBS in this word grid below?

A	A	C	A	Y	V	X	G	U	P	R	S	S	U	K
S	Y	E	I	Y	F	O	R	U	M	J	M	O	O	R
T	B	R	I	G	H	T	O	N	A	A	T	W	S	I
O	M	D	P	U	E	B	M	A	N	C	I	T	Y	T
N	U	S	N	F	Y	P	F	I	U	U	E	N	R	O
V	C	A	P	I	N	E	O	R	N	M	W	C	X	T
I	O	D	K	F	V	J	P	U	I	Z	I	H	I	T
L	I	V	E	R	P	O	O	L	T	D	A	E	X	E
L	E	I	C	E	S	T	E	R	E	T	S	L	A	N
A	A	M	X	V	T	Y	T	D	D	E	F	S	C	H
C	R	Y	S	T	A	L	P	A	L	A	C	E	Q	A
W	E	S	T	H	A	M	A	R	S	E	N	A	L	M
A	F	W	Z	B	K	O	T	F	A	O	M	V	B	M
O	E	N	U	D	Q	M	R	E	V	E	R	T	O	N

- ★ ARSENAL
- ★ ASTON VILLA
- ★ BRIGHTON
- ★ CHELSEA
- ★ CRYSTAL PALACE
- ★ EVERTON
- ★ LEICESTER
- ★ LIVERPOOL
- ★ MAN. CITY
- ★ MAN. UNITED
- ★ TOTTENHAM
- ★ WEST HAM

GUESS WHO!

Name these high-profile ENGLAND STARS from these OLD photos!

1

NAME:..................................

2

NAME:..................................

3

NAME:..................................

4

NAME:..................................

ANSWERS ON PAGE 92! **91**

ANSWERS!

How did you get on with the QUIZZES?
It's time for you to find out!

BADGES AND ANIMALS!

ON P9

1 B West Brom, 2 C Oxford, 3 A Leicester, 4 C Gillingham,
5 A Cardiff, 6 B Millwall, 7 C Norwich, 8 C Aston Villa, 9 A Watford

A YEAR IN FOOTBALL!
ON P20

1 B, 2 A, 3 B, 4 B, 5 C, 6 C, 7 B, 8 A, 9 C

CRISTIANO RONALDO QUIZ!
ON P30-31

1 C, 2 B, 3 A, 4 B, 5 C, 6 B, 7 C, 8 A, 9 B, 10 C

GUESS WHO?
ON P61

1 Jordan Pickford, 2 Cole Palmer, 3 Ella Toone,
4 Bruno Guimaraes, 5 Pedro Porro, 6 Marcus Rashford,
7 John McGinn, 8 Ben White, 9 Lauren James

QUIZ AN ADULT!

ON P73-77

1 A Emmanuel Petit; B Marc Overmars, 2 D, 3 A Paul McGrath;
B Ryan Giggs, 4 A Aston Villa; B Southampton; C Oldham,
5 Tottenham, 6 A Yes; B No; C Yes; D No, 7 Chris Waddle,
8 Steve McMahon, 9 Portsmouth, 10 A Stuart Pearce; B Des Walker,
11 C, 12 B, 13 C, 14 D, 15 D, 16 C, 17 D, 18 C, 19 C, 20 A

SPOT THE BALL!

ON P90-91

BALL 1 1C   BALL 2 1F   BALL 3 1G   BALL 4 1F

WSL CLUBS WORDSEARCH!

A	A	C	A	Y	V	X	G	U	P	R	S	S	U	K
S	Y	E	I	Y	F	O	R	U	M	J	M	O	O	R
T	B	R	I	G	H	T	O	N	A	A	T	W	S	I
O	M	D	P	U	E	B	M	A	N	C	I	T	Y	T
N	U	S	N	F	Y	P	F	I	U	U	E	N	R	O
V	C	A	P	I	N	E	O	R	N	M	W	C	X	T
I	O	D	K	F	V	J	P	U	I	Z	I	H	I	T
L	I	V	E	R	P	O	O	L	T	D	A	E	X	E
L	E	I	C	E	S	T	E	R	E	T	S	L	A	N
A	A	M	X	V	T	Y	T	D	D	E	F	S	C	H
C	R	Y	S	T	A	L	P	A	L	A	C	E	Q	A
W	E	S	T	H	A	M	A	R	S	E	N	A	L	M
A	F	W	Z	B	K	O	T	F	A	O	M	V	B	M
O	E	N	U	D	Q	M	R	E	V	E	R	T	O	N

GUESS WHO!

1 Leah Williamson, 2 Alex Greenwood, 3 Beth Mead, 4 Lauren Hemp

MATCH OF THE DAY MAGAZINE

Telephone 020 7150 5513
Email inbox@motdmag.com

Editor   Mark Parry
Deputy Editor   Jake Wilson
Art Editors   Bradley Wooldridge, John Leonard
Features Editor   Sarah Johnson
Production Editor   Will Demetriou
Writer   Ollie Spencer

Freelance Designers   Pete Rogers, Alastair Par
Acting Commercial Director   Rachel Clare
Group Editor   Richard Clare
Assistant Publisher   Igrain Roberts
Annual images   Getty Images

BBC Books is an imprint of Ebury Publishing. One Embassy Gardens. 8 Viaduct Gardens. London SW11 7BW.
BBC Books is part of the Penguin Random House group of companies whose addresses can be found at global.
penguinrandomhouse.com. Copyright © Match of the Day Magazine 2024. First published by BBC Books in 2024.
www.penguinrandomhouse.co.uk. A CIP catalogue record for this book is available from the British Library.
ISBN 9781785948381. Commissioning Editor: Albert DePetrillo Project Editor: Shammah Banerjee Production: Phil Spencer.
Printed and bound in Italy by Elcograf S.p.A. The authorised representative in the EEA is Penguin Random House Ireland.
Morrison Chambers. 32 Nassau Street. Dublin 2. Penguin Random House is committed to a sustainable future for our
business our readers and our planet. This book is made from Forest Stewardship Council ® certified paper.

BBC

BBC Match Of The Day Magazine is published by Immediate Media Company
London Limited under licence from BBC Studios Distribution Limited.
© Immediate Media Company London Limited 2024.

NIGERIA

No.
10
Icon

JAY JAY
OKOCHA

AUGUSTINE AZUKA 'JAY-JAY' OKOCHA

2025 FOOTY BINGO!

TICK THESE *mad predictions off as they happen... if any happen!*

Erling Haaland rocks a multi-coloured moustache!

Chelsea sign Paddington Bear for £150m!

Harry Kane scores 100 goals in 50 games!

Lionel Messi retires to raise owls!

Man. United add bucket hats to their kit!

Adam La Llama wins the Ballon d'Or!